SCOTT HAHN'S STUDY GUIDE FOR

THE LAMB'S SUPPER

Also by Scott Hahn

The Lamb's Supper: The Mass as Heaven on Earth

Hail, Holy Queen: The Mother of God in the Word of God

First Comes Love: Finding Your Family in the Church and the Trinity

Lord, Have Mercy: The Healing Power of Confession

Swear to God: The Promise and Power of the Sacraments

Letter and Spirit: From Written Text to Living Word in the Liturgy

*Reasons to Believe: How to Understand, Explain, and Defend the
    Catholic Faith*

*Ordinary Work, Extraordinary Grace: My Spiritual Journey in
    Opus Dei*

Signs of Life: 40 Catholic Customs and the Difference They Make

Understanding the Scriptures: A Complete Course on Bible Study

*Scripture Matters: Essays on Reading the Bible from the Heart of the
    Church*

Understanding "Our Father": Biblical Reflections on the Lord's Prayer

A Father Who Keeps His Promises: God's Covenant Love in Scripture

Rome Sweet Home: Our Journey to Catholicism
    (with Kimberly Hahn)

Living the Mysteries: A Guide for Unfinished Christians
    (with Mike Aquilina)

The Catholic Bible Dictionary (General Editor)

STUDY GUIDE FOR

THE LAMB'S SUPPER

SCOTT HAHN

IMAGE BOOKS / DOUBLEDAY RELIGION

New York London Toronto Sydney Auckland

IMAGE

An Image Book

Copyright © 2010 by Scott W. Hahn

All Rights Reserved

Published in the United States by Image Books/Doubleday Religion, an imprint of the Crown Publishing Group, a division of Random House, Inc., New York.
www.crownpublishing.com

IMAGE, the Image colophon, and DOUBLEDAY are registered trademarks of Random House, Inc.

Nihil Obstat: Monsignor Michael F. Hull, STD, Censor Librorum
Imprimatur: Most Reverend Dennis J. Sullivan, Auxiliary Bishop and Vicar General, Archdiocese of New York

The *Nihil Obstat* and *Imprimatur* are official declarations that a book or pamphlet is free of doctrinal or moral error. No implication is contained therein that those who have granted the *Nihil Obstat* or *Imprimatur* agree with the content, opinions, or statements expressed.

Library of Congress Cataloging-in-Publication Data
   Hahn, Scott.
      Study guide for the Lamb's Supper / Scott Hahn.—1st ed.
         p.   cm.
      Includes bibliographical references.
1. Hahn, Scott. Lamb's Supper.   2. Mass.   3. Lord's Supper—Biblical teaching.   4. Bible. N.T. Revelation—Theology.   5. Catholic Church—Doctrines.   I. Title.
   BX2230.3.H35   2010
264.0203607—dc22   2010009194

ISBN 978-0-307-58905-7

PRINTED IN THE UNITED STATES OF AMERICA

First Edition

Contents

Preface   [13]

How to Use This Book   [19]

STUDY SESSION 1
Foreword by Father Benedict Groeschel, C.F.R.   [21]

STUDY SESSION 2
**Introduction—Christ Stands at the Door:
The Mass Revealed**   [26]

STUDY SESSION 3
**Part 1, Chapter 1—In Heaven Right Now: What I Found
at My First Mass**   [32]

STUDY SESSION 4
**Part 1, Chapter 2—Given for You:
The Story of Sacrifice**   [37]

STUDY SESSION 5

Part 1, Chapter 3—From the Beginning: The Mass of the
First Christians   [44]

STUDY SESSION 6

Part 1, Chapter 4—Taste and See (and Hear and Touch)
the Gospel: Understanding the Parts of the Mass   [50]

STUDY SESSION 7

Part 2, Chapter 1—"I Turned to See": The Sense amid
the Strangeness   [57]

STUDY SESSION 8

Part 2, Chapter 2—Who's Who in Heaven: Revelation's
Cast of Thousands   [64]

STUDY SESSION 9

Part 2, Chapter 3—Apocalypse Then! The Battles of
Revelation and the Ultimate Weapon   [70]

STUDY SESSION 10

Part 2, Chapter 4—Judgment Day: His Mercy
Is Scary   [77]

STUDY SESSION 11

Part 3, Chapter 1—Lifting the Veil: How to See
the Invisible   [83]

STUDY SESSION 12

Part 3, Chapter 2—Worship Is Warfare: Which Will You
Choose: Fight or Flight?   [90]

STUDY SESSION 13

Part 3, Chapter 3—Parish the Thought: Revelation as
Family Portrait   [97]

STUDY SESSION 14

Part 3, Chapter 4—Rite Makes Might: The Difference
Mass Makes   [103]

SCOTT HAHN'S STUDY GUIDE FOR

THE LAMB'S SUPPER

Preface

The millennium was waning, and a variety of folks—
from televangelists to computer scientists—were wring-
ing their hands over what might come at the end of the
countdown. As the calendar rolled over to 2000 (Y2K,
for the headline writers' convenience), would the super-
computers go haywire and the power grid crash? Would
Christ come upon the clouds and rapture up the Christians, leaving the remaining rabble to descend into moral
and material chaos? If you channel-surfed the television
for a few minutes, you could gather many conflicting an-
swers to those questions.

I was no stranger to such speculation. I was born into a
mainline Protestant family. As a teen I underwent a deep
conversion and gravitated toward evangelical Christianity. As an adult I was ordained to the ministry and served
as a pastor and teacher. Those were the years when books
like *The Late, Great Planet Earth* sold tens of millions of
copies. It was a religious culture in which you could

identify yourself by your opinions about the last book of the Bible, the Book of Revelation. There were many options, and those who held them had long since hardened into factions. Were you a dispensationalist? A premillennialist or postmillennialist? An amillennialist? A preterist? It *mattered*. As the millennium wound down, many people considered it a matter of life and death.

Like so many of my fellow evangelicals, I was studying the Book of Revelation closely, intensely, and prayerfully. I immersed myself in the history of interpretation. And it was that study that led me to an unexpected place: the Roman Catholic Church.

As the year 2000 approached, I had been a Catholic for a decade and a half, and I had watched millennium fever spread even to some folks in the Catholic Church. Influenced by evangelical pop culture, they felt tremendous anxiety about the tribulations that now seemed inevitable and imminent. These were the days when the Left Behind series, a fictionalized rendering of the "Last Days," was enjoying sales in the millions.

Thus, when Doubleday approached me and asked if I would be interested in writing a book, I didn't hesitate to answer yes. The Catholic Church had a consistent and compelling interpretation of the Book of Revelation; and, unlike the prediction industry, the Church hadn't changed its understanding to fit the passing events. History vindicated the saints again and again.

The ancient Fathers believed that the Book of Revelation presented an icon of the liturgy—the Mass—the Church's ritual public worship. This doesn't mean that it was irrelevant to historical events. It means that the liturgy is the key to understanding historical events.

So, while Catholics have always cultivated a healthy sense of awe about the Mass, we have been spared the disordered fear of the "end times." The message of the Book of Revelation is the message we were hearing, in those premillennial days, from Pope John Paul II: "Be not afraid."

We believe in the real presence of Jesus Christ in the Holy Eucharist. Thus, since the first generation of Christianity, we have lived in joyful expectation of his coming in glory, his *Parousia*. We believe that a world is indeed, and always, coming to an end; but that is good news, because a better world awaits us. We begin to live in that new creation—in the Kingdom of God, in heaven!—even now, as we live out our Eucharistic lives on earth.

Yet so many Catholics were missing out on this message, distracted instead by interpretive schemes devised by people who could not see the liturgical sense of the Apocalypse, because they had never known the liturgy.

I was eager to write *The Lamb's Supper*. I believed there was a need for it.

I was not, however, prepared for what followed. Rather quickly, the book sold out in its first printing. At one point it shot to number-five ranking on Amazon, passing Harry Potter and other epic best sellers along the way. The Eternal Word Television Network (EWTN) asked if I would appear on a thirteen-week series of interviews based on the book; and I did.

Then the stories started coming in from readers. There were conversions of people who had struggled for years to make sense of Revelation's puzzling imagery and oracles. The star quarterback of an NCAA Division I football team contacted me to let me know that after reading *The Lamb's Supper* he had made the decision to enter the seminary. (He has since been ordained to the priesthood.) A group of U.S. bishops invited me to lead their annual retreat. A pontifical university in Rome invited me to teach a course based on the book. Hardly a day went by without an invitation to speak at some parish or conference.

I was gratified. I was stunned. I was humbled. I went before the Lord with tears to thank him.

It all happened so quickly, I hardly had time to absorb it. But the full realization came, quite suddenly, one day as I was walking through the Philadelphia airport.

As I approached my gate, a young boy approached me. "Are you Dr. Scott Hahn?" he asked.

He told me he was eleven and a half years old, and he recognized my face from the television series *The Lamb's Supper*. He wanted me to know that he was then reading my book for the *second* time. The first time through, he had started to attend daily Mass. His father, who was with him, chimed in that now Junior had the rest of the family going to Mass along with him!

If I never sold another book, I think I could have been satisfied with that brief exchange. The book did, however, go on to reach hundreds of thousands of people. Through the years, many have asked me to produce a study guide, so that they could study the book in discussion groups, in their parishes and homes. Now, ten years after that first publication, my publisher, too, is asking for a book about the book. So here it is. For each chapter I asked a friend of mine, Mike Aquilina, to provide questions for discussion. Since Mike asked all the questions in the original *Lamb's Supper* television series, I thought this task might come easily to him!

I have no right to ask anything of you. You have already been generous in giving me your attention. But consider me a beggar at your door as I urge you to pursue your reading and discussion in prayer. When we speak of the Mass, we are venturing into the Holy of Holies, where God would have us live with him.

Know God's presence, then, as you discuss the Mass as heaven on earth; and, in his presence, speak always with charity, especially when you speak of his priests or the Church's liturgy—but also when you speak of the choir, the lectors, the cantors, and your fellow worshippers. Let your discussion be a form of prayer, and let it rise like incense before the Lord.

I ask you, too, when you pray, to pray for me.

—Scott Hahn
Feast of the Epiphany of Our Lord 2010

How to Use This Book

You may use the book in any way you wish. For each session I have indicated a chapter of the book for advance reading. I have supplemented this "assignment" with pointers to other supplementary material—from the Bible, from the *Catechism of the Catholic Church*, and from other Church documents. I have also chosen, for each session, a hymn whose text is related to the discussion at hand. Singing sometimes loosens up the voices of discussion group members. And these traditional hymns will certainly give you something to talk about.

But my outline here is not intended to be a ritual. You're free to use the elements that appeal to you and your group, in whatever order you please. You may skip whatever doesn't work for you.

Foreword by Father Benedict Groeschel, C.F.R.

SUMMARY AND KEY POINTS

- This book brings together several powerful spiritual realities.
- Eschatology is the study of "last things."
- It is important that we conduct our study with a proper sense of the sacraments.

At my invitation, Father Benedict Groeschel wrote a foreword to *The Lamb's Supper*. Father Benedict approaches the subject of the book from a very different perspective. He is a priest and I'm a layman. Father Benedict is a "cradle Catholic" and I'm a convert. Yet we converge upon a common faith; and, for very different reasons, we see a clear relationship between three realities that many people see as distinct or even unrelated: the Mass, the end times, and the Book of Revelation.

Father Benedict emphasizes the contrast between his

own experience and mine. For me, the book is all about exciting "discoveries" I made in my studies. For him, the book is about an everyday reality he has known since he was an altar boy. These elucidations are not a novelty to him, but rather what he has "thought about the Eucharist for decades."

Father Benedict also emphasizes certain things that are distinctive about Catholic doctrine and practice. He refuses, for example, to classify the Mass as a religious "service," preferring terms such as "Divine Liturgy" instead. Similarly, he speaks of his own priesthood as a share in the priesthood of Christ, who is our only true priest.

He is especially concerned with the "sacramental" quality of the Church's worship. According to tradition, a sacrament is an outward sign, instituted by Christ and entrusted to the Church. Through signs that can be perceived by the senses, the sacraments bestow divine grace.

Father Benedict notes that many people are disturbed by the prospect of the end of time, but he is himself at ease with the possibility of its fulfillment in his lifetime or its indefinite delay.

Along the way, he introduces us to certain key terms, such as *eschatology*, a theological term that refers to the study of last things. He encourages us to study "carefully" and "learn."

SCRIPTURE

Revelation 4:8–11; 5:9–14; 7:10–12; 19:1–8

DOCTRINE

Catechism of the Catholic Church, n. 2642: The *Revelation* of "what must soon take place," the *Apocalypse,* is borne along by the songs of the heavenly liturgy but also by the intercession of the "witnesses" (martyrs). The prophets and the saints, all those who were slain on earth for their witness to Jesus, the vast throng of those who, having come through the great tribulation, have gone before us into the Kingdom, all sing the praise and glory of him who sits on the throne, and of the Lamb. In communion with them, the Church on earth also sings these songs with faith in the midst of trial. By means of petition and intercession, faith hopes against all hope and gives thanks to the "Father of lights," from whom "every perfect gift" comes down. Thus faith is pure praise.

SONG

COME, DIVINE INTERPRETER
By Charles Wesley

(To the tune of "For the Beauty of the Earth")

> Come, divine Interpreter,
> Bring me eyes your book to read,
> Ears the mystic words to hear,
> Words which did from you proceed,
> Words that endless bliss impart,
> Kept in an obedient heart.

All who read, or hear, are blessed,
If your plain commands we do;
Of your kingdom here possessed,
You we shall in glory view
When you come on earth to abide,
Reign triumphant at your side.

QUESTIONS FOR REFLECTION AND DISCUSSION

1. Before reading this book, had you ever connected the Mass with the end times and the Book of Revelation? Had anyone ever made the connection for you?

2. How, do you think (or would you guess), are these three things related?

3. Is your own experience of the Mass closer to that of Father Benedict Groeschel or that of the author of this book? Or does your experience share elements of both? Explain your answer.

4. How do you feel about the possibility of the world ending? What hopes or fears does it arouse in you?

5. What, do you think, separates a sacrament from a mere "service" of the sort Father Benedict mentions?

6. What will you look for in your study of "the end times"—your study of eschatology? What are your

interests, concerns, expectations, or worries about the climax of history?

7. Have you ever had an experience at Mass that you considered a glimpse or foretaste of heaven? Has anyone you know had such an experience?

Introduction

Christ Stands at the Door
The Mass Revealed

SUMMARY AND KEY POINTS

- The Mass is familiar, but it contains hidden mysteries.
- The Book of Revelation (or Apocalypse) seems strange, but it contains familiar things.
- The Mass is heaven on earth.

The Lamb's Supper is divided into three parts, and Part One, titled "The Gift of the Mass," begins with two verses from the Book of Revelation. Jesus is standing and knocking at a door, and then the door opens up for John the Seer, the author of the Apocalypse. Presumably, it opens for us as well, those with whom John shares his visions.

We begin our considerations by contrasting the familiarity of the Mass with the strangeness of the Bible's Apocalypse. In *The Lamb's Supper*, I mention some of the more bizarre details of Revelation, and we see just how off-putting the visions can be. We understand why some readers are scared away.

We then encounter the idea of the Mass as "heaven on earth," as stated by Pope John Paul II and the ancient Catholic tradition. I recount how I came to that realization late, at the end of a long search to find a "key" to the Book of Revelation.

This might seem counterintuitive. Maybe your lived experience of Mass stands in stark contrast to the most common ideas about heaven. Yet I insist, throughout the book, that we do go to heaven when we go to Mass "regardless of the quality of the music or the fervor of the preaching."

There are many ways we might study the Book of Revelation—or any book of the Bible. *The Lamb's Supper*, however, focuses on only one aspect or dimension. The book is not a commentary, a Bible study, or a how-to manual. It is more a meditative introduction to a single mystery in the Church's life: the Mass as heaven on earth. That mystery is "unveiled" in a partial way in the Book of Revelation. The faithful will see it as it is when their earthly lives draw to a close and they go to heaven.

The terminology in the book arises from my own experience as a Catholic Christian of the Western Church, the Latin Rite. The Church has many rites, however, and the central idea of *The Lamb's Supper*—and of the Book of Revelation—applies equally to each and all.

SCRIPTURE

Revelation 3:20; 4:1

DOCTRINE

Pope John Paul II, *Ad Limina* Address to the Bishops of Washington, Oregon, Idaho, Montana, and Alaska, October 9, 1998, nn. 2, 5: The challenge now is to . . . reach the proper point of balance, especially by entering more deeply into the contemplative dimension of worship, which includes the sense of awe, reverence and adoration which are fundamental attitudes in our relationship with God. This will happen only if we recognize that the liturgy has dimensions *both* local *and* universal, time-bound *and* eternal, horizontal *and* vertical, subjective *and* objective. It is precisely these tensions which give to Catholic worship its distinctive character. The universal Church is united in the one great act of praise; but it is always the worship of a particular community in a particular culture. It is the eternal worship of Heaven, but it is also steeped in time. It gathers and builds a human community, but it is also "the worship of the divine majesty" (*Sacrosanctum Concilium* 33). . . . At the core of this experience of pilgrimage is our journey as sinners into the unfathomable depths of the Church's liturgy, the liturgy of Creation, the liturgy of Heaven. . . . That is the purpose of all our worship and all our evangelizing.

Catechism of the Catholic Church, n. 1203: The liturgical traditions or rites presently in use in the Church are the

Latin (principally the Roman rite, but also the rites of certain local churches, such as the Ambrosian rite, or those of certain religious orders) and the Byzantine, Alexandrian or Coptic, Syriac, Armenian, Maronite, and Chaldean rites. In "faithful obedience to tradition, the sacred Council [Vatican II] declares that Holy Mother Church holds all lawfully recognized rites to be of equal right and dignity, and that she wishes to preserve them in the future and to foster them in every way."

SONG

ALL HAIL THE POWER OF JESUS' NAME
By Edward Perronet

All hail the power of Jesus' name!
Let angels prostrate fall;
Bring forth the royal diadem,
And crown him Lord of all.
(Repeat last 2 lines.)

Crown him, ye martyrs of our God
Who from his altar call;
Extol the stem of Jesse's rod,
And crown him Lord of all.
(Repeat last 2 lines.)

Ye chosen seed of Israel's race,
A remnant weak and small,
Hail him who saves you by his grace,
And crown him Lord of all.
(Repeat last 2 lines.)

Ye Gentile sinners, ne'er forget
The wormwood and the gall;
Go, spread your trophies at his feet
And crown him Lord of all.

(Repeat last 2 lines.)

Babes, men, and sires, who know his love,
Who feel your sin and thrall,
Now join with all the hosts above,
And crown him Lord of all.

(Repeat last 2 lines.)

Let every kindred, every tribe
On this terrestrial ball,
To him all majesty ascribe,
And crown him Lord of all.

(Repeat last 2 lines.)

O that, with yonder sacred throng,
We at his feet may fall!
We'll join the everlasting song,
And crown him Lord of all.

(Repeat last 2 lines.)

QUESTIONS FOR REFLECTION AND DISCUSSION

1. Have the strange details of the Book of Revelation intrigued you or put you off till now? Explain.

2. What has been your experience of non-Catholic readings of the Book of Revelation? Have you read

them? Have others "witnessed" them to you? What did you think?

3. What do you make of the drive of many non-Catholics to understand the last book of the Bible? What object could motivate *you* to make such a search?

4. Why might studying the Book of Revelation be worth an extraordinary effort?

5. What parts of the Mass make you feel most "at home"?

6. What circumstances regularly distract your attention from the Mass?

7. Have you attended the liturgies of other "rites" of the Catholic Church? Did they emphasize the heavenly aspects of worship in ways that had been unfamiliar to you? What do you remember most vividly from those experiences?

Part 1, Chapter 1

In Heaven Right Now
What I Found at My First Mass

SUMMARY AND KEY POINTS

- A stranger at Mass will find many scriptural surprises.
- The language of eschatology, the visions of Revelation, are often liturgical in content.
- *Parousia,* the term often applied to the Second Coming, has other meanings.

I hope you enjoy my trip down memory lane. To launch *The Lamb's Supper,* I take you along to the first Mass I ever witnessed. At the time I was a young Protestant minister studying for a doctoral degree in theology. I had been reading the works of the early Church Fathers, and their frequent discussions of the liturgy aroused my curiosity.

Still, I'd been trained to believe that the Mass was "idolatry," so I feared my curiosity might be a temptation to sin.

I decided to "sneak" into a weekday Mass and observe from a distance. I brought my Bible with me and flipped through the pages as (to my surprise) I recognized the scriptural prayers, readings, and allusions scattered throughout the ritual. Gradually, I discovered what you, perhaps, already know: that the Mass is saturated with Scripture, from both the Old Testament and the New Testament. I found, too, that the Mass focused entirely on the God I had always loved and worshipped: the God of Abraham and Isaac, the God revealed in Jesus Christ, the Blessed Trinity.

Gradually, I was drawn into the drama of the liturgy, as it moved from the proclamation to the sacrifice. I became less a spectator and more a participant. But it was the Mass's Communion Rite, with its repeated invocation of Jesus as the "Lamb of God," that planted me squarely in a very familiar place: *in the pages of the Book of Revelation.* In the Apocalypse, I knew, Jesus appeared as a lamb and was repeatedly addressed as the Lamb of God.

I returned to Mass again and again. My observations in the chapel propelled me into further and deeper study of the ancient Fathers as well as the Church's Councils. All this compelled me to return to the Scriptures and to read them as the Fathers did and as the Church had always read them. In the pages of the Bible, I "discovered" one Catholic doctrine and practice after another—only to learn that my "discoveries" had been commonplaces of the early Church, devoutly held by theologians and unlettered peasants.

I learned also that my observations had been confirmed by Protestant biblical scholars. My experience of Catholic worship changed the way I pursued my theological studies. Meanwhile, my theological studies changed the way I approached divine worship. These changes would bring about a bigger change in my life: my conversion to Catholicism and reception into full communion with the Church.

SCRIPTURE

Hebrews 12:18–19, 22–24

DOCTRINE

Catechism of the Catholic Church, n. 1090: "In the earthly liturgy we share in a foretaste of that heavenly liturgy which is celebrated in the Holy City of Jerusalem toward which we journey as pilgrims, where Christ is sitting at the right hand of God, Minister of the sanctuary and of the true tabernacle. With all the warriors of the heavenly army we sing a hymn of glory to the Lord; venerating the memory of the saints, we hope for some part and fellowship with them; we eagerly await the Savior, our Lord Jesus Christ, until he, our life, shall appear and we too will appear with him in glory."

St. Irenaeus of Lyons (second century), *Against Heresies* 4.18.6: It is [God's] will that we, too, should offer a gift at the altar, frequently and unceasingly. The altar, then, is in heaven, for towards that place our prayers and oblations are directed; the temple likewise is there, as John says in the Revelation, "Then God's temple in heaven was opened" (Revelation 11:19). "Behold," he says, "the dwelling of God is with men" (Revelation 21:3).

SONG

O LORD, I AM NOT WORTHY
By Irvin Udulutsch, OFM Cap., and others

O Lord, I am not worthy
That thou should'st come to me,
But speak the words of comfort,
My spirit healed shall be.

Oh, come, all you who labor
In sorrow and in pain,
Come, eat this bread from heaven;
Thy peace and strength regain.

O Jesus, we adore thee,
Our victim and our priest,
Whose precious Blood and Body
Become our sacred feast.

O sacrament most holy,
O sacrament divine!
All praise and all thanksgiving
Be ev'ry moment thine.

QUESTIONS FOR REFLECTION
AND DISCUSSION

1. Why do you suppose some non-Catholics fear that the Mass might be "idolatry"?

2. What impressed Dr. Hahn most about the Mass he attended?

3. How was he persuaded, gradually, that the Mass was true worship?

4. Think of your non-Catholic friends and family members. What kinds of impressions would they have if they "dropped in" on a Mass in a nearby church?

5. What can you do to welcome strangers at Mass?

6. How do you imagine the "Second Coming" of Jesus? Does it change anything for you to think about it as his Real Presence in the Mass?

7. Some people complain that Catholic worship has an inadequate sense of "community," because it is so much focused on God. Do you think these circumstances helped or hindered Dr. Hahn in his search for true worship?

For Further Reading

Scott Hahn, *Swear to God: The Promise and Power of the Sacraments* (New York: Doubleday, 2003), chapters 1–2.

Part 1, Chapter 2

Given for You
The Story of Sacrifice

SUMMARY AND KEY POINTS

- A lamb makes an unlikely hero, yet it was the centerpiece of Israel's sacrificial worship.
- Sacrifice has many meanings and accomplishes and expresses many things.
- The New Testament presents our salvation in terms of sacrifice, Passover, and the Lamb.

At the beginning of this chapter we consider the "lamb" as a symbol of the Savior and Son of God—a symbol that seems odd and inappropriate. Compared to Jesus' other titles, this one seems to lack dignity. A lamb is an animal not particularly intelligent or strong. Yet the title is applied to Jesus twenty-eight times in the Book of Revelation, and at least four or five times in an ordinary Mass!

Devotion to Jesus as "the Lamb" is central to the Bible's Apocalypse and to the Mass. In order to understand this devotion, however, we must first understand the function of sacrifice in biblical religion. For the lamb was a sacrificial offering.

This chapter traces the "story of sacrifice" through human history. The story begins with the first offerings of Cain and Abel, and continues throughout the early history of mankind and Israel: bread and wine offered by the priest Melchizedek, and the burnt offerings of Abraham and Isaac and Jacob. God called for a unique and important sacrifice when he asked Abraham to offer his beloved son, Isaac. Because of Abraham's faithfulness, God blessed him and promised to bless his descendants.

God's promises and blessings to Abraham were later invoked by Moses and applied to Israel during the exodus from Egypt. Israel was liberated from slavery by God's miraculous intervention at the first Passover. A plague swept through the land, claiming every firstborn in Egypt, but the Israelite families were spared because the Passover lambs were offered, as God had instructed, in place of the Israelites' firstborn sons.

When the kingdom of Israel was established, the sacrifice continued in the Jerusalem Temple, which God intended to be a house of prayer for all nations.

The Old Testament tells of characters and events that are historically true; but in God's plan they also *foreshadow* or *prefigure* history's ultimate fulfillment in Jesus Christ. In theological language, the Old Testament sacrifices are "types"; and Jesus' sacrifice marks their fulfillment.

What does sacrifice accomplish? In this chapter we

examine several "ends" of sacrifice, all drawn from the biblical narratives. Sacrificial worship recognizes God's sovereignty over life and over all creation; it gives thanks; it solemnly seals a covenant oath; it expresses renunciation and sorrow for sins.

The Passover was a pivotal sacrifice in Israel's history. In the time of Christ, Jerusalem would be thronged for the feast every year. More than a quarter million lambs would be sacrificed every year at Passover. The Passover Seder, a solemn ritual meal, was obligatory, not optional; it was the way individuals and families renewed their covenant with God.

The Gospel writers use the language of Passover to describe both Jesus' Last Supper and his crucifixion. The sacrificial lamb fits the divine pattern of our salvation.

SCRIPTURE

Exodus 12:1–23; Luke 22:1, 7–1; John 1:36, 19:36; 1 Corinthians 5:7–8; Revelation 5:6

DOCTRINE

Catechism of the Catholic Church, n. 1085: In the liturgy of the Church, it is principally his own Paschal mystery that Christ signifies and makes present. During his earthly life Jesus announced his Paschal mystery by his teaching and anticipated it by his actions. When his Hour comes, he lives out the unique event of history which does not pass away: Jesus dies, is buried, rises from the dead, and is seated at the right hand of the Father "once for all." His Paschal mystery is a real event that occurred in our history, but it is unique: all other historical events happen once, and then they pass away, swallowed up in the past. The Paschal mystery of Christ, by contrast, cannot remain only in the past, because by his death he destroyed death, and all that Christ is—all that he did and suffered for all men—participates in the divine eternity, and so transcends all times while being made present in them all. The event of the Cross and Resurrection *abides* and draws everything toward life.

Catechism of the Catholic Church, n. 1104: Christian liturgy not only recalls the events that saved us but actualizes them, makes them present. The Paschal mystery of Christ is celebrated, not repeated. It is the celebrations that are repeated, and in each celebration there is an outpouring of the Holy Spirit that makes the unique mystery present.

SONG

PANIS ANGELICUS
By St. Thomas Aquinas

At this our solemn feast
Let holy joys abound,
And from the inmost breast
Let songs of praise resound;

Let ancient rites depart,
And all be new around,
In every act, and voice, and heart.

Now we recall that eve,
When, the Last Supper spread,
Christ, as we all believe,
The Lamb, with leav'nless bread,
Among his brethren shared,
And thus the Law obeyed,
Of all unto their sires declared.

Now, with the Lamb consumed,
The legal Feast complete,
The Lord unto the Twelve
His Body gave to eat;
The whole to all, no less
The whole to each did mete
With His own hands, as we confess.

He gave them, weak and frail,
His Flesh, their food to be;
On them, downcast and sad,
His Blood bestowèd he:
And thus to them he spake,
"Receive this cup from me,
And all of you of this partake."

So he this Sacrifice
To institute did will,
And charged his priests alone
That office to fulfill:

To them he did confide:
To whom it pertains still
To take, and the rest divide.

Thus angels' Bread is made
The Bread of man today:
The living Bread from heaven
With figures dost away:
O wondrous gift indeed!
The poor and lowly may
Upon their Lord and Master feed.

QUESTIONS FOR REFLECTION AND DISCUSSION

1. Some people say that all love requires sacrifice. What sacrifices do we make for earthly loves? What do these sacrifices teach us about sacrifice offered to God?

2. What reasons might God have for commanding animal sacrifice?

3. Think about the several reasons given for offering sacrifice. Which ones, would you say, apply to your experience of worship? What purposes for offering sacrifice do you hear in the Liturgy of the Eucharist?

4. How did the many Old Testament sacrifices prepare the way for the one sacrifice of Jesus Christ? Why do the Gospels apply the language of the Passover to both the Last Supper and the crucifixion?

5. Why does Jesus' sacrifice put an end to the sacrifices of the Jerusalem Temple? Without an earthly Temple, how does Christ extend his sacrifice through time?

6. Why does the Lamb in Revelation appear to be slain, though he is alive?

7. Consider Mohandas Gandhi's claim that "religion without sacrifice" is an absurdity of the modern age. Why is such a conception of religion absurd? Why should sacrifice be an integral part of religious life?

For Further Reading

Scott Hahn, *Swear to God: The Promise and Power of the Sacraments* (New York: Doubleday, 2003), chapter 3.

Scott Hahn, *Letter and Spirit: From Written Text to Living Word in the Liturgy* (New York: Doubleday, 2005), chapter 6.

Part 1, Chapter 3

From the Beginning
The Mass of the First Christians

SUMMARY AND KEY POINTS

- Some elements of the Church's rites have deep roots in the liturgy of Israel.
- From the Church's beginning, Mass was central to the practice of Christianity.
- We can recognize our Mass in the Masses of our earliest spiritual ancestors.

In this chapter we examine the ritual of the Mass as it developed from the worship of ancient Israel—and then developed through the history of the Church. We learn that Jesus kept a certain continuity with Israel's forms; and we discuss two in particular: the *todah,* or thank offering, and the Seder, or Passover meal. Some elements of these rites have "passed over" into the Catholic Church's celebration of the Mass.

Yet Jesus has transformed the ancient "types" by fulfilling them. What was once foreshadowed is now revealed in the candlelight of the Mass.

So we return to that pivotal moment in the history of the rites of God's people, and we examine the "institution narrative" that is embedded in three of the Gospels (Matthew, Mark, and Luke) and one of the New Testament epistles (1 Corinthians). At the Last Supper, Jesus took bread, blessed it, broke it, and pronounced it to be his body; he took a cup of wine and pronounced it to be his blood. Then he commanded his disciples to "do this" in memory of him. The New Testament shows that they did as they had been told. The history of the Church shows that Christians, ever after, followed that example. We still do today.

The Mass was the central and defining ritual of the ancient Church. Everywhere Christianity spread, we find evidence of its celebration. This chapter cites many examples of this historical fact, but I concentrate especially on the earliest years, the generations and centuries immediately after the time of the apostles. The Mass is at the heart of the *Didache*, a document of the first century. By the time St. Ignatius of Antioch began writing his letters, shortly after A.D. 100, Christianity had a richly developed theology of the Eucharist, which the bishop applied effortlessly to matters of life and discipline in the Church.

Christians celebrated the Mass and loved the Mass. Pagans, however, often misunderstood the nature of Christian worship. They accused members of the Church of cannibalism, because they spoke of eating the flesh of Christ and drinking his blood.

By A.D. 150, St. Justin felt the need to write a detailed account of the Mass for the edification of the Roman emperor and the senate. I include that account in its entirety in chapter 3—as did the recent *Catechism of the Catholic Church*—because it accurately describes the Mass even in our own day!

This chapter provides an account of the further development of Christian rites as the faith spread to different lands and language groups and cultures. The more inessential matters changed, the more the basic rite stayed the same.

SCRIPTURE

Luke 22:7–20, 24:13–35; Acts 2:42; 1 Corinthians 11:23–31

DOCTRINE

Catechism of the Catholic Church, n. 1346: The liturgy of the Eucharist unfolds according to a fundamental structure which has been preserved throughout the centuries down to our own day. It displays two great parts that form a fundamental unity:

- the gathering, the liturgy of the Word, with readings, homily, and general intercessions;

- the liturgy of the Eucharist, with the presentation of the bread and wine, the consecratory thanksgiving, and communion.

The liturgy of the Word and liturgy of the Eucharist together form "one single act of worship"; the Eucharistic table set for us is the table both of the Word of God and of the Body of the Lord.

Catechism of the Catholic Church, n. 1347: Is this not the same movement as the Paschal meal of the risen Jesus with his disciples? Walking with them he explained the Scriptures to them; sitting with them at table "he took bread, blessed and broke it, and gave it to them" (Luke 24:13–35).

SONG

LET ALL MORTAL FLESH KEEP SILENCE
By Gerard Moultrie

Let all mortal flesh keep silence,
And with fear and trembling stand;
Ponder nothing earthly minded,
For with blessing in His hand,
Christ our God to earth descendeth,
Our full homage to demand.

King of kings, yet born of Mary,
As of old on earth he stood,
Lord of lords, in human vesture,

In the Body and the Blood;
He will give to all the faithful
His own self for heavenly food.

Rank on rank the host of heaven
Spreads its vanguard on the way,
As the Light of light descendeth
From the realms of endless day,
That the powers of hell may vanish
As the darkness clears away.

At His feet the six-wingèd seraph,
Cherubim with sleepless eye,
Veil their faces to the Presence,
As with ceaseless voice they cry:
Alleluia, Alleluia,
Alleluia, Lord Most High!

QUESTIONS FOR REFLECTION AND DISCUSSION

1. What do you find most interesting about the early accounts of the Mass?

2. The rituals of Israel, the Passover Seder and the *todah* sacrifice, prefigured our celebration of the Mass. Consider each of these and identify their implications and emphases. How might they influence our prayer and worship today?

3. If you could travel back in time, do you think you would know what to do at a first- or second-century

Mass? Would a first- or second-century Christian know what to do at your parish this Sunday?

4. The pagans of the ancient world thought the Mass was an act of ritual cannibalism. How is the Mass commonly misunderstood today?

5. Do you think our situation is better or worse than that of our spiritual ancestors? Explain.

6. The Mass has survived for two thousand years with its basic form intact. It is one of very few institutions that have survived that long. What, do you think, has enabled it to endure while civilizations have risen and fallen?

7. Why do you suppose the *Catechism,* published in 1994, used a text from A.D. 150 to describe the Mass today? Why not just produce something new?

For Further Reading

Scott Hahn, *Letter and Spirit: From Written Text to Living Word in the Liturgy* (New York: Doubleday, 2005), chapter 1.

Part 1, Chapter 4

Taste and See (and Hear and Touch) the Gospel
Understanding the Parts of the Mass

SUMMARY AND KEY POINTS

- Ritual is an important part of human life.
- The parts of the Mass are rich in symbolic meaning and historical significance.
- The Mass is a profoundly biblical way to worship.

Here we look at the basic structure of the Mass and its constituent parts. For some readers, this may be a remedial chapter, but it's rich material that we can always stand to review, even to the end of our days. Those who are familiar with the makeup of the Mass may gain some "new" insights from the reflections of the saints and the witness of the Scriptures.

The chapter opens with a defense of ritual—which is perhaps necessary in an age that prizes novelty and spontaneity over habit and form. Yet form and habit serve us well in many important areas of our lives. We should not be so quick to discard time-honored routines from life's most important dimensions: the religious and spiritual. Human nature has not changed since A.D. 33. Christians have always lived by certain disciplines. The Church has always observed certain obligations. We are wise to keep them. We ignore them at our peril.

In the book, I tell the story about one of my first experiences of the Church's ritual prayer. It was during a visit to a Byzantine Rite seminary. With incense and chant and icons, the prayers engaged many of my senses. That day I realized "why God gave me a body." This is an important insight about liturgical prayer. The Mass involves our senses, purifies them, and elevates them. Our whole body glorifies the Lord.

What follows next in chapter 4 is a step-by-step tour of the Mass and its various postures, gestures, and prayers. I sketch their scriptural roots and their development through Christian history, and I examine the meaning behind the Mass's many symbols. This kind of teaching, used by the Church since ancient times, is called *mystagogy* (pronounced *MIST-uh-go-gee*). It comes from a Greek word meaning "guidance in the mysteries." The Catholic Church has been calling insistently for a rediscovery of the methods of mystagogy (see the "doctrine" section on the following page).

In the course of this chapter, we read about the profound meaning of such ingrained Catholic habits as making the Sign of the Cross. We learn about the relationship between ritual repentance and Holy Communion. We learn the meaning of such prayers as the Gloria and the Creed. We discover the forgotten Eucharistic meaning of the Lord's Prayer. We learn about the connection between the Church's reverence for the Bible and its love of the Mass. Even such small details as the mixing of water and wine are deeply symbolic; the Church is trying to tell us something important during every moment we spend at worship.

This chapter also gives us practical tips for praying the Mass, offering everything in life—our work and home and leisure—along with the bread and wine as we "consecrate the world itself to God."

SCRIPTURE

Acts 20:7; 1 Corinthians 10:17; Hebrews 12:18–24

DOCTRINE

Catechism of the Catholic Church, n. 1075: Liturgical catechesis aims to initiate people into the mystery of Christ (the "mystagogy") by proceeding from the visible to the invisible, from the sign to the thing signified, from the "sacraments" to the "mysteries."

Pope Benedict XVI, the February 22, 2007, post-synodal apostolic exhortation *Sacramentum Caritatis,* n. 64: [M]ystagogy . . . should always respect three elements:

a) *It interprets the rites in the light of the events of our salvation,* in accordance with the Church's living tradition. The celebration of the Eucharist, in its infinite richness, makes constant reference to salvation history. In Christ crucified and risen, we truly celebrate the one who has united all things in himself (cf. Ephesians 1:10). From the beginning, the Christian community has interpreted the events of Jesus' life, and the Paschal Mystery in particular, in relation to the entire history of the Old Testament.

b) A mystagogical catechesis must also be concerned with *presenting the meaning of the signs* contained in the rites. This is particularly important in a highly technological age like our own, which risks losing the ability to appreciate signs and symbols. More than simply conveying information, a mystagogical catechesis should be capable of making the faithful more sensitive to the language of signs and gestures which, together with the word, make up the rite.

c) Finally, a mystagogical catechesis must be concerned with bringing out the *significance of the rites for the Christian life* in all its dimensions—work and responsibility, thoughts and emotions, activity and repose. Part of the mystagogical process is to demonstrate how the mysteries celebrated in the rite are linked to the missionary responsibility of the faithful. The mature fruit of mystagogy is an awareness that one's life is being progressively transformed by the holy mysteries being celebrated. The aim of all Christian education, moreover, is to train the believer in an adult faith that can make him a "new creation," capable of bearing witness in his surroundings to the Christian hope that inspires him.

SONG

LORD, ACCEPT THE GIFTS
Sr. M. Teresine Haban, O.S.F.

Lord, accept the gifts we offer
At this Eucharistic feast:
Bread and wine to be transformed now
Through the action of your priest
Take us, too, Lord, and transform us.
May your grace in us increase.

May our souls be pure and spotless
As the host of wheat so fine;
May all stain of sin be crushed out,
Like the grape that forms the wine,
As we too become partakers
In this sacrifice divine.

Take our gifts, almighty Father,
Living God, eternal, true,
Which we give through Christ, our Savior,
Pleading here for us anew.
Grant salvation to all present,
And our faith and love renew.

QUESTIONS FOR REFLECTION
AND DISCUSSION

1. Do you sense a dramatic "flow" or development in the way the Mass proceeds? If you had to outline your experience of the Mass, what parts would you highlight? Why?

2. From the New Testament onward, the Church has always observed the Mass in two parts: the Liturgy of the Word and the Liturgy of the Eucharist. Why do you think Jesus established it this way?

3. In what ways does the Mass engage your body and senses? What does this do for your spirit?

4. What does it mean to "consecrate the world itself to God"? How might this take place in the Mass?

5. As you read this chapter, did you learn anything new about old familiar parts of the Mass? If so, which parts? And why do you think you missed their meaning till now?

6. What is your attitude toward ritual? What is your attitude toward spontaneity? Can a healthy spiritual life incorporate both? Should it?

7. Why do you think the Church has so insistently emphasized the need for a recovery of the methods of mystagogy—guidance in the mysteries of our ritual worship?

For Further Reading

Scott Hahn, *Letter and Spirit: From Written Text to Living Word in the Liturgy* (New York: Doubleday, 2005), chapters 2 and 9.

Scott Hahn, *Swear to God: The Promise and Power of the Sacraments* (New York: Doubleday, 2003), chapter 11.

Part 2, Chapter 1

"I Turned to See"
The Sense amid the Strangeness

SUMMARY AND KEY POINTS

- Revelation's oddities must be confronted.
- Many readers propose ways to make sense of the imagery of the Apocalypse.
- A Catholic, liturgical reading enables the most coherent reading of the Book of Revelation.

This chapter begins Part Two, "The Revelation of Heaven." Our focus shifts from a familiar sanctuary— that of our parish church—to one that is maybe less familiar: the sanctuary of heaven depicted in the Book of Revelation. As we move from one to the other, we follow St. John the Seer, the author of the Apocalypse, who was worshipping in the spirit on the Lord's day when he "turned to see" (Revelation 1:12) his visions.

We should not shrink from the strangeness of those visions—the plagues and beasts and infestations . . . invasions of seemingly demonic armies . . . and angel defenders wielding previously unknown weapons—chalices. Reading Revelation, we encounter consuming fires, rivers of blood, streets paved with gold. We see long-haired locusts who have human faces, lion's teeth, scorpion's tails, and are crowned with golden diadems.

Such details are many and strange, and they defy our conventional tools of logical or literary analysis. How should we begin to make sense of them? Some commentators, such as Martin Luther, have just given up and denied that the book belongs in the Bible!

Here we are introduced to several interpretive schemes: "futurists" who think the Apocalypse is simply (or mostly) an encoded prediction of specific future events; "idealists" who think the book is mostly a metaphor for the struggles and triumphs of the spiritual life; and "preterists," who believe that Revelation is a stylized description of events that were important for the first-century Church.

Each of these schemes presents us with a partial truth and seems to solve a portion of the puzzle. Each, however, falls short in some respects. In *The Lamb's Supper* I note some weaknesses of the various schools of thought. Futurists grow cynical when several projected doomsdays pass by and the end times need to be recalculated—or the "beasts" they identify leave office after uneventful terms.

Others lose sight of the forest because of their fascination with one tree or another. The millennium occupies only a small portion of the text of Revelation, but it has filled the imagination of recent readers. Sometimes the interpretations tell us more about the interpreters than about the text.

Instead of fixating on single points in isolation of all others, let's look for a common thread or theme. As I point out in the book, we'll find such a motif in the liturgical details of John's visions: the prayers and readings, vestments, altar, candles, incense, hymns, and chants.

I invite you to try an imaginative exercise: let's pretend we are Greek-speaking Jewish Christians who were the first readers of the Apocalypse. For them, the Jerusalem Temple was God's sanctuary, designed to reflect heavenly realities in an earthly way. The Temple, however, was destroyed when the Romans crushed the Judean revolt in A.D. 70. What were God's people to make of this?

Christians knew that Jesus had identified himself as God's temple (see John 2:19–21), and Jesus had identified himself with his people, the Church (see Acts 9:4). So the Temple was no longer merely a building in Jerusalem. God intended the rituals of the Jerusalem Temple to foreshadow the worship under the New Covenant. The former temple now found its fulfillment in Jesus' body, the Church, and its sacred liturgy, carried out according to Jesus' command.

SCRIPTURE

1 Corinthians 3:16–17; 2 Corinthians 6:16; Ephesians 2:19–22

DOCTRINE

Cardinal Francis Arinze, "The Holy Eucharist Unites Heaven and Earth," Address at Eucharistic Congress in Washington, D.C., September 25, 2004: The Apocalypse, or the Book of Revelation, as it [is] also known, presents a striking imagery of the heavenly liturgy and helps us appreciate how the Eucharistic celebration, as it were, looks heavenward. At the same time, the Eucharist commits us to do our part to make this world a better place in which to live. Indeed, the Eucharist unites heaven and earth and calls for our active faith response. . . .

The Book of Revelation speaks in prophetic and apocalyptic language with the Jerusalem temple worship as background. But it also speaks of the Church beginning to spread in the world and presents Jesus Christ as the Gospel Lamb, the King of the universe, the High Priest, the Lord of history and the immaculate Victim on his throne.

In the Apocalypse, divine worship is praise of heaven begun on earth. The cult images are powerful and clearly liturgical. Examples are adoration of the immolated Lamb on His throne, hymns and canticles, acclamations of the crowds of the elect dressed in white, descent of the Church of heaven on earth, the Jerusalem of which the Lord Jesus is the temple. And the people are a priestly and royal one. The visions recall many cult elements: seven candlesticks, the long white robe of the Son of Man, the white dress of the old men and of the Saints, the altar, the Amen and the exultant Alleluia.

At the same time the Book of Revelation also describes the exasperation of the fight between hell and the faithful of Christ, between the Woman and her children and

the Beast, the false prophet who would do all in his power
to seduce the inhabitants of the world.

The Eucharist is linked with this heavenly liturgy and,
if well celebrated and lived on earth, will inaugurate the
reign of God and dismiss the Devil and his angels.

SONG

HOLY, HOLY, HOLY
By Reginald Heber

Holy, holy, holy! Lord God Almighty!
Early in the morning our song shall rise to thee;
Holy, holy, holy, merciful and mighty!
God in three Persons, blessed Trinity!

Holy, holy, holy! All the saints adore thee,
Casting down their golden crowns around the
    glassy sea;
Cherubim and seraphim falling down before thee,
Who were, and are, and evermore shall be.

Holy, holy, holy! though the darkness hide thee,
Though the eye of sinful man thy glory may not
    see;
Only thou art holy; there is none beside thee,
Perfect in power, in love and purity.

Holy, holy, holy! Lord God Almighty!
All thy works shall praise thy name, in earth and
    sky and sea;

Holy, holy, holy! Merciful and mighty!
God in three Persons, blessed Trinity!

QUESTIONS FOR REFLECTION AND DISCUSSION

1. Have you ever been attracted to any of the various interpretive strategies outlined in *The Lamb's Supper*—the futurist, for example, or the preterist, or the idealist? If so, why?

2. Have you known Christians who were deeply affected by their reading of the Apocalypse? How did it change their life in the short term? How did it change their life in the long term?

3. Why do you think God chose to reveal himself in such strange and shocking terms? What does it accomplish?

4. How might the Church's tradition be helpful in resolving difficulties in reading the Bible?

5. Have you ever been truly frightened by a passage or book of the Bible? Why? How did you resolve your fears?

6. With the fall of the Jerusalem Temple, the early Christians saw a "world" coming to an end. What events in history—or in your life—have been comparable to this? What do these experiences suggest about how we understand the end of the world?

7. If you were living in the Church's first generation, would the Apocalypse have brought you comfort or consolation? Why or why not? What does your answer suggest about the application of the Book of Revelation to life today?

For Further Reading

Scott Hahn, *Hail, Holy Queen: The Mother of God in the Word of God* (New York: Doubleday, 2001), chapter 3.

Part 2, Chapter 2

Who's Who in Heaven
Revelation's Cast of Thousands

SUMMARY AND KEY POINTS

- Revelation's drama depends, to some extent, on how we identify its characters.
- Key characters are the Lamb, the Woman, the Bride, and the beasts.
- Some of these characters may have multiple identifications.

We begin this chapter by noting that Revelation is the "most populous book in the Bible," encompassing all the peoples of the earth, and all the spirits in heaven and hell.

Yet certain characters stand out from the crowd, and they are sketched rather vividly. There is the author, of course, who identifies himself four times as John. And there is the Lamb, who is the pivotal figure in the drama, the object of the expectation of his people, and the focus of their worship. At the midpoint of the visions, there is a woman, especially graced and gifted by God, crowned and clothed with celestial lights. She gives birth to the Messiah and lives in constant peril from the threats of his enemies.

Then there are the beasts—grotesque in their appearance, terrifying in their power. They have been a point of fascination for readers in recent years. Who are these monsters? There is a popular and sensationalist tendency, especially among futurists, to identify the beasts with political candidates or rulers of whom they disapprove. People have "decoded" one or another beast as Napoleon, Bismarck, Hitler, Stalin, and even Ronald Wilson Reagan, whose misfortune it was to have exactly six letters in each of his three names.

It is helpful here to revisit an idea we discussed earlier: that of typology, the study of biblical "types." A type is a person, place, event, or precept that is historically true, but is also a foreshadowing, to be fulfilled at a later time or in eternity. Often a type is representative of a pattern in history. A theologian once observed that prophecy is simply the typological view of history. Prophecy is the application of the biblical models to contemporary and coming events.

Thus, John's vision of beasts may have represented imperial Rome for first-century Christians—but, nevertheless, it reveals a truth that is more universal, and it may be equally applicable to a twenty-first-century government, or an earthly power still far in the future.

Amid the crowds of the Apocalypse we encounter angels, martyrs, virgins, priests, who cry out from around the altar and whose prayers rise from bowls of incense. Where but in Catholic tradition can we find a way to make sense of all the roles of all these people? Catholic churches still keep the relics of the martyrs encased in the earthly altars. Catholics still consecrate themselves to lives of celibacy and virginity. Catholics still venerate the angels and observe their feast days. Catholicism is the one place where all these details come together in a sensible way.

SCRIPTURE

Revelation 5:8–14; 11:19–12:1–6; 14:1–5

DOCTRINE

Catechism of the Catholic Church, n. 1136: Liturgy is an "action" of the *whole Christ* (*Christus totus*). Those who even now celebrate it without signs are already in the heavenly liturgy, where celebration is wholly communion and feast.

Catechism of the Catholic Church, n. 1187: The liturgy is the work of the whole Christ, head and body. Our high priest celebrates it unceasingly in the heavenly liturgy, with the holy Mother of God, the apostles, all the saints, and the multitude of those who have already entered the kingdom.

SONG

HOLY GOD, WE PRAISE THY NAME
By Ignaz Franz (translated by Clarence A. Walworth)

Holy God, we praise thy name;
Lord of all, we bow before thee!
All on earth thy scepter claim,
All in heaven above adore thee;
Infinite thy vast domain,
Everlasting is thy reign.
(Repeat last 2 lines.)

Hark! the loud celestial hymn
Angel choirs above are raising;
Cherubim and seraphim,
In unceasing chorus praising;
Fill the heavens with sweet accord:
Holy, holy, holy Lord.
(Repeat last 2 lines.)

Lo! the apostolic train
Join the sacred name to hallow;
Prophets swell the loud refrain,
And the white-robed martyrs follow;
And from morn to set of sun,
Through the Church the song goes on.
(Repeat last 2 lines.)

Holy Father, Holy Son,
Holy Spirit, Three we name thee;
While in essence only one,
Undivided God we claim thee;

And adoring bend the knee,
While we own the mystery.
(Repeat last 2 lines.)

QUESTIONS FOR REFLECTION
AND DISCUSSION

1. Have you ever seen contemporary figures identified with the beasts of Revelation? Why did commentators make such an association? What reasons
   does a Catholic have for avoiding this practice?

2. The Church has, down the centuries, identified the
   "woman" of Revelation 12 with the Blessed Virgin
   Mary. What, do you think, are the consequences of
   this for Christian life and prayer?

3. The author of the Apocalypse identifies himself
   four times as "John," and the early Church Fathers
   believed that the visions provided the key to inter-
   preting John's Gospel. How can the Book of Revelation help us to read the life of Jesus with greater
   understanding?

4. Why does the Apocalypse give such a prominent
   role to the martyrs and consecrated virgins? Why
   does the Church continue to venerate such Christians?

5. Why do you think the same figure, Jesus, appears in
   Revelation as a lamb, a lion, a light, and a "Son of
   Man"? What can the vision teach us about him?

6. What do you think the numbers represent? Actual population figures? Symbolic associations? Give reasons.

7. The people discussed in Revelation seem to fall into two categories: Israel and the "nations" ("Gentiles"). Why does John make this distinction? How is it significant in the drama of Revelation—and the drama of history?

Part 2, Chapter 3

Apocalypse Then!
The Battles of Revelation and the Ultimate Weapon

SUMMARY AND KEY POINTS

- Revelation presents history and life as a great battle.
- The warfare depicted refers to historical battles, but also to spiritual realities.
- Jerusalem, the holy city, is an important key to our understanding of the Book of Revelation.

The drama of the Book of Revelation turns on the outcome of battles. The seer describes them in obviously allegorical terms, so it is easy to look upon them as metaphors for our spiritual struggles. Yet he also provides rather precise geographical locations and hints at other on-the-ground historical details. So we are drawn to conclude that an exclusively allegorical reading of the text may produce an overly simplistic interpretation— one that ignores historical reality.

The battle of Armageddon, as it plays out in the Apocalypse, has always cast a spell of fascination over readers. Its scale is epic. Its consequences are—everything. It is a world war and still an otherworldly war.

We ground ourselves in the interpretive tradition by explaining the literal and spiritual senses of Scripture. The literal sense is foundational, and it must be affirmed before we proceed to any allegorical or spiritual reading. No true spiritual interpretation can contradict the literal sense of Scripture. Nevertheless, we face special difficulties when we're reading a book whose literal sense is itself an allegory; so we need to make a special effort to sort these out.

John the Seer informs us that the events he describes will happen "soon." And history seems to corroborate his hunch. The second half of the first century was a violent period for John, his kin, and his Church. Nero launched a bloody persecution of Christians, and Domitian built on Nero's precedent. The Jews in Palestine split into bloody and fratricidal factions as they rebelled against Roman government. The Romans responded by laying siege to the holy city and starving its residents—before burning the city, leveling it, and expelling the Jews from the land.

The people of Israel could look back on a long history of military campaigns—including both victories and defeats. They knew that battles were never simply earthly. God and his angels were always involved, and the outcome always implied a divine judgment rendered. John's visions follow in that tradition. He seems to allude to first-century events, but he places them in the context of eternity, of judgment and providence.

He situates action in the Jerusalem he knew, but flashes backward in time to Jericho, Egypt, and other battle sites. Armageddon, the plain of Megiddo near Jerusalem, is itself the site of a historic defeat.

Jerusalem is judged for its sin, which is compared to marital infidelity—prostitution and fornication. Yet we must never read this as a blanket condemnation of Jews, Judaism, or Israel. Anti-Judaism and anti-Semitism are incompatible with Christian faith. First-century Jerusalem received a judgment that has also been visited upon many Christian cities through subsequent history. It is interesting to note that all the seven churches addressed in the Book of Revelation have essentially vanished—suppressed by Muslim invaders during the first millennium.

The destruction of Jerusalem marks not just an ending, but a beginning, a renewed covenant þetween God and man. No longer would God's intimate presence be confined to a single sanctuary. Now it would be everywhere, in his Church, where he abides in the Eucharist.

This sacrament we celebrate as Christ's real presence, and that is the literal meaning of the Greek word *parousia*. Christ comes to us in the Mass; he remains with us in the tabernacle.

At Mass, believers receive hidden manna for sustenance. They are "sealed" off from their enemies by the Sign of the Cross. In the Apocalypse, these facts emerge in stark contrast to certain historical details: the starvation that killed the besieged inhabitants of the earthly Jerusalem; the Roman legions that crushed the city to rubble.

SCRIPTURE

Revelation 11, 17–19

DOCTRINE

Catechism of the Catholic Church, n. 409: This dramatic situation of "the whole world [which] is in the power of the evil one" makes man's life a battle:

> The whole of man's history has been the story of dour combat with the powers of evil, stretching, so our Lord tells us, from the very dawn of history until the last day. Finding himself in the midst of the battlefield man has to struggle to do what is right, and it is at great cost to himself, and aided by God's grace, that he succeeds in achieving his own inner integrity.

Catechism of the Catholic Church, n. 410 After his fall, man was not abandoned by God. On the contrary, God calls him and in a mysterious way heralds the coming victory over evil and his restoration from his fall. This passage in Genesis is called the *Protoevangelium* ("first gospel"): the first announcement of the Messiah and Redeemer, of a battle between the serpent and the Woman, and of the final victory of a descendant of hers.

SONG

PRAISE TO THE LORD
By Joachim Neander (translated by Catherine Winkworth)

Praise to the Lord, the Almighty, the King of
   creation!
O my soul, praise him, for he is your health and
   salvation!
All you who hear, now to his altar draw near,
Praise him in glad adoration.

Praise to the Lord, who, when tempests and
   warfare are waging,
Who, when the elements madly around thee are
   raging,
Bids them to cease, turns all their fury to peace,
Whirlwinds and waters assuaging.

Praise to the Lord, who, when darkness of sin is
   abounding,
Who, when the godless do triumph, all virtue
   confounding,
Then sheds his light, chases the horrors of night,
Saints with his mercy surrounding.

Praise to the Lord, O let all that is in me adore
   him!

All that has life and breath, come now with praises
   before him!
Let the Amen sound from his people again,
Now as we worship before him.

QUESTIONS FOR REFLECTION
AND DISCUSSION

1. What are the possible benefits or drawbacks of preferring a perennial view of Revelation to the popular futurist interpretations?

2. What are we to make of the fact that St. Thomas
   Aquinas and St. Augustine found Revelation diffi-
   cult to interpret? Is this grounds for despair or consolation?

3. Why does John pose riddles and draw heavy-handed
   allegories instead of stating matters plainly?

4. Why would John compare the holy city, Jerusalem,
   to such places as Egypt and Sodom? What is he say-
   ing about Jerusalem's morals and its relationship
   with God?

5. What might the fall of Jerusalem in A.D. 70 mean to
   a Jewish Christian? A Gentile Christian? A pagan?
   A non-Christian Jew? What should that long-ago
   event mean to us today?

6. What do you make of the fall of all those ancient
   Christian churches? How do our own churches
   measure up to the descriptions of these churches in
   the opening chapters of the Book of Revelation?

7. Why does Dr. Hahn call anti-Semitism "spiritual stupidity"? Why does the Church condemn it? How can we avoid this trap the devil springs on some Christians?

For Further Reading

Scott Hahn, *Letter and Spirit: From Written Text to Living Word in the Liturgy* (New York: Doubleday, 2005), chapters 7 and 9.

Part 2, Chapter 4

Judgment Day
His Mercy Is Scary

SUMMARY AND KEY POINTS

- People mistakenly believe God's mercy is incompatible with his "wrath."
- Mercy and justice are complementary aspects of God's love.
- We can better understand God's mercy and justice in light of parental discipline.

So much of the Book of Revelation is concerned with God's judgment of the world. We see that God is just, and he pronounces severe sentence upon the wicked. We see, too, that he is merciful, and he rewards the righteous.

Some of Christianity's critics, however, look at the Bible's teachings and tell us that we can't have it both ways. God is either just or he is merciful, they say; he cannot be both.

But the Book of Revelation shows us that God cannot be just unless he is also merciful, and he cannot be perfectly merciful unless he is also just. His justice and mercy are simply two sides of the same fatherly love.

Now we explore what we really mean when we call God "Father." We are his children because he has established a sacred family bond with us. That is the very meaning of "covenant," as we see in both the Old and New Testaments.

Family life always observes some order—some set of assumptions, protocols, and customs that we observe unquestioningly. When we violate these conventions, we can find ourselves at odds with our own family.

In a covenant family, sin is more than a broken law. It is a broken relationship, a broken home. God administers a justice that is restorative, medicinal, remedial. He wants to mend what is broken and reunite those who have strayed from the family home. Sometimes he administers what seems to be a "punishment" in order to wake us up, or warn us away from spiritual dangers, or help us break away from things we might prefer to him.

Yet he respects our freedom, and if we insist on doing things that separate us from him and his covenant family, he will respect our decision. He will not love us any less. But, as a consequence of our own choice, we will find his love unbearable. We will find his love loathsome. The same fire that warms heaven for the saints can only be hell for sinners.

Even in this life, we can misjudge events when we judge them by a purely human standard. When "bad" things happen to good people, they are actually good things, because they enable the faithful to grow in virtue and become more Christ-like in their suffering. When "good" things happen to bad people, they are actually bad things, because they can make it easier for them to remain in sin.

This is a basic truth of Christianity. When St. Paul spoke of the Mass, he pointed out that the same cup that brought blessing to the faithful brought death to sinners (see 1 Corinthians 11:29–32).

We should be attentive: we are always in God's presence. When we approach Holy Communion, we are drawing near to the fire of God's love.

SCRIPTURE

Revelation 15 and 16

DOCTRINE

Catechism of the Catholic Church, n. 1040: The Last Judgment will come when Christ returns in glory. Only the Father knows the day and the hour; only he determines the moment of its coming. Then through his Son Jesus Christ he will pronounce the final word on all history. We shall know the ultimate meaning of the whole work of creation and of the entire economy of salvation and understand the marvellous ways by which his Providence led everything towards its final end. The Last Judgment will reveal that God's justice triumphs over all the injustices committed by his creatures and that God's love is stronger than death.

Catechism of the Catholic Church, n. 1041: The message of the Last Judgment calls men to conversion while God is still giving them "the acceptable time, . . . the day of salvation" (2 Corinthians 6:2). It inspires a holy fear of God and commits them to the justice of the Kingdom of God. It proclaims the "blessed hope" of the Lord's return, when he will come "to be glorified in his saints, and to be marvelled at in all who have believed" (Titus 2:13; 2 Thessalonians 1:10).

SONG

DAY OF WRATH
By Thomas of Celano (translated by Sir Walter Scott)

(To the tune of "O Saving Victim")

> That day of wrath, that dreadful day,
> When heav'n and earth shall pass away!
> What pow'r shall be the sinner's stay?
> How shall he meet that dreadful day?
>
> When, shriveling like a parchèd scroll,
> The flaming heav'ns together roll;

When louder yet, and yet more dread;
Swells the high trump that wakes the dead.

O on that day, that wrathful day
When man to judgment wakes from clay,
Be thou the trembling sinner's stay,
Though heav'n and earth shall pass away.

QUESTIONS FOR REFLECTION
AND DISCUSSION

1. Why do parents discipline their children? What do they hope to gain by the process? What does this suggest to us about God's fatherly discipline?

2. What happens to mercy that is devoid of justice? What happens to justice devoid of mercy?

3. In what sense is hell the guarantor of human freedom? Can we truly love someone if we do not have the freedom to reject them?

4. If God is unchanging, what do we mean when we speak of his "wrath"?

5. Why is God's love bliss for some and unbearable for others? Why does the same fire warm the righteous and burn the wicked?

6. In the course of your life, have you ever experienced a disaster or seeming tragedy that, in some way, proved to be your salvation?

7. Angels clearly play an important role in God's governance over the world. What role do they play in your life and your devotion?

For Further Reading

Scott Hahn, *Lord, Have Mercy: The Healing Power of Confession* (New York: Doubleday, 2003), chapter 6.

Part 3, Chapter 1

Lifting the Veil
How to See the Invisible

SUMMARY AND KEY POINTS

- Behind the symbols of the Mass are the mysteries of heaven.
- This chapter's helpful chart shows where elements of the Mass appear in Revelation.
- The Apocalypse depicts the symbolic "wedding" of heaven and earth in Jesus Christ.

The third and final section of the book, "Revelation for the Masses," begins with this chapter and the story of the emissaries of Prince Vladimir of Kiev. After attending their first Christian liturgy, they declared: "We did not know whether we were in heaven or on earth."

It was an aesthetic experience, a delight to the senses.

But that's not all it was. The sensory experience was sacramental. It was an outward sign of an inner, invisible presence.

So we return to an idea we encountered in Study Session 6, the idea of mystagogy, or guidance in the mysteries. Mystagogy is the method we can use to go beyond the sacramental signs, to perceive the divine mysteries that await us in eternity. Cardinal Joseph Ratzinger (who would later become Pope Benedict XVI) said that in the Mass we experience the "already" entering the "not yet."

Heaven, after all, is nothing less than our unending communion with God. Yet we experience heaven already in the Mass. When Christ comes in his fullness, he will not possess any more glory than he possesses on our altars. The difference is that in heaven we will see him as he is. *We* will be changed.

Still, we enter that glory now. We consume it. We possess it. That is fundamental Christian doctrine, as we see in the Church's official documents.

Chapter 1 of Part 3 includes a detailed chart showing which parts of the Mass appear in the Book of Revelation. Read this closely, and you'll see the Mass in the small details of the Apocalypse, but it is also reflected in the grand scheme of the Book of Revelation. As the Mass is divided into two parts, the Liturgy of the Word and the Liturgy of the Eucharist, so the Apocalypse is divided into two parts: the first depicts the reading of the letters and the breaking of the seal, and the second is the marriage supper of the Lamb.

The marriage supper is clearly the culmination of the drama, and it may be reflected in the very title of the biblical book. *Apokalypsis* is Greek for "unveiling," an event that marked the climax of the weeklong wedding celebrations of the Jews in the first century. The unveiling of the bride denoted the consummation of the marriage. Thus, the Apocalypse somehow marks the consummation of the bond between Christ and his bride, the Church.

In the second half of the Book of Revelation, we see the consequences of this marriage of heaven and earth. The veil has been rent. Angels and humanity now join together in common worship. When John begins to bow down before an angel, the angel lifts him up.

We must learn to look with new eyes at what we've been missing, what was once veiled to our sight, and to see the spiritual realities as they are revealed to us—in the Book of Revelation, in the Mass, in our relationship with Jesus Christ, in our hardships, in our joys, and in every moment of life.

SCRIPTURE

Ephesians 5:21–23; Revelation 19:1–9, 21:1–10

DOCTRINE

Catechism of the Catholic Church, n. 1111: Christ's work in the liturgy is sacramental: because his mystery of salvation is made present there by the power of his Holy Spirit; because his Body, which is the Church, is like a sacrament (sign and instrument) in which the Holy Spirit dispenses the mystery of salvation; and because through her liturgical actions the pilgrim Church already participates, as by a foretaste, in the heavenly liturgy.

Pope John Paul II, the April 17, 2003, encyclical *Ecclesia de Eucharistia,* n. 19: This is an aspect of the Eucharist which merits greater attention: in celebrating the sacrifice of the Lamb, we are united to the heavenly "liturgy" and become part of that great multitude which cries out: "Salvation belongs to our God who sits upon the throne, and to the Lamb!" (Revelation 7:10). The Eucharist is truly a glimpse of heaven appearing on earth. It is a glorious ray of the heavenly Jerusalem which pierces the clouds of our history and lights up our journey.

SONG

BRIDE OF CHRIST
By Herbert S. Oakeley

(To the tune of "Ode to Joy")

> Bride of Christ, whose glorious warfare
> Here on earth hath never rest;
> Lift thy voice, and tell the triumphs
> Of the holy and the blest;
> Joyous be the day we hallow,
> Feast of all the saints on high,
> Earth and heav'n together blending
> In one solemn harmony.

First the blessèd virgin mother,
Reunited to her Son,
Leads the host of ransomed people,
Who unfading crowns have won;
John, the herald, Christ's forerunner,
More than prophet, leads his throng,
Seer and patriarch responsive
Unto psalmist in their song.

Lo, the twelve, majestic princes,
In the court of Jesus sit,
Calmly watching, while the conflict
Rages far beneath their feet;
Lo, the martyrs, robed in crimson,
Sign of life blood freely spent,
Finding life, because they lost it,
Dwell in undisturbed content.

All the saintly host who witnessed
Good confessions for his sake—
Priest and deacon, world renouncing,
Of their Master's joy partake;
Virgins to the Lamb devoted,
Following with steadfast love,
Bring their lilies and their roses
To the marriage feast above.

All, their happy lot fulfilling,
God omnipotent proclaim;
Holy, holy, holy, crying,
Glory to his holy Name!
So may God in mercy grant us

Here to serve in holiness,
Till he call us to the portion
Which his saints in light possess.

QUESTIONS FOR REFLECTION
AND DISCUSSION

1. What makes liturgy beautiful? Is it the poetry, music, art, architecture, incense—all of the above? Or is it something that the senses cannot perceive?

2. If the ritual of the Mass is meant to express heavenly realities, what kinds of art, architecture, and music are appropriate to the occasion?

3. How can music and homilies be better employed to convey the meaning of the Mass? Can they, too, be occasions of mystagogy?

4. What does it mean to say that marriage is a sacrament (or sign) of Christ's communion with the Church? What does the sacramental nature of marriage imply for the day-to-day living of a married couple?

5. What changes in our lives if we believe that our time in heaven begins right now? What should change?

6. What can we do to heighten our awareness of Jesus' *Parousia* when we receive Holy Communion?

7. What can we do to help our friends and families become more aware of what's invisible in the Mass?

For Further Reading

Scott Hahn, *Swear to God: The Promise and Power of the Sacraments* (New York: Doubleday, 2003), chapter 14.

Scott Hahn, *Letter and Spirit: From Written Text to Living Word in the Liturgy* (New York: Doubleday, 2005), chapters 2 and 9.

Part 3, Chapter 2

Worship Is Warfare
Which Will You Choose: Fight or Flight?

SUMMARY AND KEY POINTS

- We find ourselves in a spiritual battle.
- For this battle, we must rethink our ideas about "power," "weakness," and "victory."
- Our victory is assured if we are faithful.

We return now to some of the themes from Study Session 9, drawing lessons from Revelation's battles and applying them to our personal struggles.

For we find that evil is everywhere, in sham imitation of God's omnipresence. It closes in on us from outside; yet we also find it emerging from our own sinful hearts. We labor so that we do not become victimized by evil. Yet we must also overcome our own inclinations, so that we do not become perpetrators of evil.

Evil—sin, rebellion against God—is what the Book of Revelation represents through its beasts and perils. Evil is what preys on innocence and spills the blood of the martyrs.

If it were not for God's mercy and grace, we would have no effective defenses against evil. So mighty are the powers of the fallen angels. So devastating is the damage original sin has wrought in our spiritual faculties.

With God's grace, though, we have hope. Indeed, we have assurance that we will prevail over evil, so long as we are faithful to the fight.

The conflict is unavoidable. We cannot opt out of the battle. To choose not to fight is to choose to be conquered by evil.

So we must learn to fight, using the techniques of spiritual combat that are hallowed by tradition. We must also learn to scout a clear view of the battlefield. This basic training should give us great confidence. We learn, for example, that when we call for help, we do receive it—every time—and we receive exactly what we need in order to emerge victorious. We don't necessarily receive exactly what we asked for. We might think that victory means escape from suffering; but God knows that our victory will come through suffering, as he modeled in his own incarnate life on earth. Consider St. Paul's account of his own spiritual fight:

> And to keep me from being too elated by the abundance of revelations, a thorn was given me in the flesh, a messenger of Satan, to harass me, to keep me from being too elated. Three times I begged the Lord about this, that it should leave me; but he said to me, "My grace is

sufficient for you, for my power is made perfect
in weakness." I will all the more gladly boast of
my weaknesses, that the power of Christ may
rest upon me. (2 Corinthians 12:7–9)

Consider, too, that the ancient Israelites prayed for
centuries for a deliverer. Yet so many did not recognize
him when he arrived, because he came according to
God's perfect will and not according to limited human
expectations.

In our struggles, in our battles, we will always receive
the help we need. All we need do is ask.

When we are weak, then we are strong. The beasts in
the Apocalypse are frightening, and they are arrayed with
their armies against a seemingly weak divine opposition:
a Lamb, a pregnant woman, a baby. Yet God's side wins.
When we fight a spiritual fight, we need to reconfigure
our ideas of strength and weakness.

In God's truth we will find peace—in the face of
history's uncertainties, in the face of evil's seeming triumph.

Worship is the most effective weapon we have. So we
must make time for worship and consecrate everything
we have to God. That leaves us less time to worry. We
don't flee from the world. We don't flee from our struggles. But we confront them in prayer, and we confront
them with prayer. We fail sometimes. But we repent and
we battle on, and we come back stronger. We already
know we are on the winning side, as long as we keep up
the fight.

The demons have nothing to withstand the weapons
God places at our disposal. We can pray. We can study.
We can receive the sacraments. We can bless ourselves

with holy water. Tradition gives us ample stores of ammunition for the good fight. We know the angels are with us. We know that they are more powerful than our opponents.

SCRIPTURE

Ephesians 6:10–17; Revelation 7

DOCTRINE

Catechism of the Catholic Church, n. 2853: Victory over the "prince of this world" (John 14:30) was won once for all at the Hour when Jesus freely gave himself up to death to give us his life. This is the judgment of this world, and the prince of this world is "cast out" (John 12:31; Revelation 12:10). "He pursued the woman" (Revelation 12:13–16) but had no hold on her: the new Eve, "full of grace" of the Holy Spirit, is preserved from sin and the corruption of death (the Immaculate Conception and the Assumption of the Most Holy Mother of God, Mary, ever virgin). "Then the dragon was angry with the woman, and went off to make war on the rest of her offspring" (Revelation 12:17). Therefore the Spirit and the Church pray "Come, Lord Jesus" (Revelation 22:17, 20), since his coming will deliver us from the Evil One.

Pope John Paul II, Address in Bulgaria, during the Pilgrimage to the Holy Monastery of Rila, Saturday, May 25, 2002: Spiritual combat . . . needs to be taught anew and proposed once more to all Christians today. It is a secret and interior art, an invisible struggle in which monks engage every day against the temptations, the evil suggestions that the demon tries to plant in their hearts; it is a combat that becomes crucifixion in the arena of solitude in the quest for the purity of heart that makes it possible to see God (cf. Matthew 5:8) and of the charity that makes it possible to share in the life of God who is love (cf. 1 John 4:16).

More than ever in the lives of Christians today, idols are seductive and temptations unrelenting: the art of spiritual combat, the discernment of spirits, the sharing of one's thoughts with one's spiritual director, the invocation of the Holy Name of Jesus and of his mercy must once more become a part of the inner life of the disciple of the Lord. This battle is necessary in order not to be distracted . . . or worried . . . (cf. 1 Corinthians 7:32, 35), and to live in constant recollection with the Lord.

SONG

FOR ALL THE SAINTS
By William Walsham How

For all the saints, who from their labors rest,
Who thee by faith before the world confessed,
Thy name, O Jesus, be forever blessed.
Alleluia, Alleluia!

O may thy soldiers, faithful, true, and bold,
Fight as the saints who nobly fought of old,
And win with them the victor's crown of gold.
Alleluia, Alleluia!

O blest communion, fellowship divine!
We feebly struggle, they in glory shine;
All are one in thee, for all are thine.
Alleluia, Alleluia!

And when the strife is fierce, the warfare long,
Steals on the ear the distant triumph song,
And hearts are brave, again, and arms are strong.
Alleluia, Alleluia!

The golden evening brightens in the west;
Soon, soon to faithful warriors comes their rest;
Sweet is the calm of paradise the blessed.
Alleluia, Alleluia!

But lo! there breaks a yet more glorious day;
The saints triumphant rise in bright array;
The King of glory passes on his way.
Alleluia, Alleluia!

From earth's wide bounds, from ocean's farthest
    coast,
Through gates of pearl streams in the countless
    host,
And singing to Father, Son and Holy Ghost:
Alleluia, Alleluia!

QUESTIONS FOR REFLECTION
AND DISCUSSION

1. What, do you think, are the most dangerous evils we must confront in our culture? Give reasons.

2. What, do you think, are the most dangerous evils we must confront in ourselves? Give reasons.

3. What practical steps can people in our circumstances take to fight the good fight daily?

4. Have you ever suffered a defeat (by worldly standards) that turned out to be a victory? Explain.

5. Have you ever taken pleasure in a victory (by worldly standards) that turned out to be a spiritual setback? Discuss, if you feel comfortable doing so.

6. What advantages do our guardian angels have in fighting with demons?

7. Have you ever been aware of the angels' assistance as you struggled spiritually or morally? How might you increase your awareness of and reliance upon the power of God's angels?

For Further Reading

Scott Hahn, *Swear to God: The Promise and Power of the Sacraments* (New York: Doubleday, 2003), chapter 11.

Part 3, Chapter 3

Parish the Thought
Revelation as Family Portrait

SUMMARY AND KEY POINTS

- The Church is a family, like the extended tribal families of ancient times.
- A covenant creates a family bond.
- The Mass simultaneously puts us in touch with Calvary and with heaven.

If we study the New Testament's doctrine of salvation, we find that Jesus and the apostles discussed it consistently in family terms. We are saved through a covenant with God—a family bond. He is our Father in heaven. We are his sons and daughters. Christ is our brother. The Church is God's family on earth; and just as in an earthly family, when we gather together for a meal we receive more than physical sustenance. The gathering together strengthens our identity and builds up a sense of common life. The Church is a *communion* because it is a family. The meal we share signifies our supernatural bond, our unity, but it also accomplishes the unity it signifies. That's what a sacrament does.

Our supernatural family, the Catholic Church, is like the big tribal families that flourished in Jesus' time. It is an extensive spiritual support network. It seals us with a distinctive signet or heraldry: the Sign of the Cross. It carries on the family name, and it blesses in that name: the Father, the Son, and the Holy Spirit.

What makes us a *supernatural* family, though, is the supernatural life we share. We share the very life of God. Baptized into Christ, we become children of God in the eternal Son of God. In communion with Christ, we live as God's children; we live as "gods" (see Psalm 82:6; John 10:34).

Such a life is, of course, impossible to our human nature. It is enabled, however, by the grace of the sacraments. Through baptism we are "partakers of the divine nature" (2 Peter 1:4). Our life in the Trinity begins at that moment, but we renew, strengthen, and intensify that bond with every Mass.

The inner life of God is self-giving, life-giving love. Its earthly image is the sacrifice of Jesus on the cross. But Jesus' sacrifice began with his incarnation, and it encompassed all the prayers, works, joys, and sufferings of his life. Everything he did was an act of love for the Father. He shares that life with us through the Mass. In the Mass, he extends his sacrifice through time.

When we receive Holy Communion, we receive the

life of Christ and—with praise and thanksgiving—accept it as our own.

Our extended family on earth is the Church, and we call our parish our home. It is there we are called to live the love that is God's nature. We must exercise patience as we live parish life, bearing with the faults and weaknesses of our fellow parishioners, our pastors, our bishops.

SCRIPTURE

Romans 12:1–5; 1 Corinthians 10:17, 13:4–7; 1 John 4:7–16

DOCTRINE

Pope John Paul II, the April 17, 2003, encyclical *Ecclesia de Eucharistia,* n. 20: Certainly the Christian vision leads to the expectation of "new heavens" and "a new earth" (Revelation 21:1), but this increases, rather than lessens, *our sense of responsibility for the world today.* I wish to reaffirm this forcefully at the beginning of the new millennium, so that Christians will feel more obliged than ever not to neglect their duties as citizens in this world. Theirs is the task of contributing with the light of the Gospel to the building of a more human world, a world fully in harmony with God's plan.

St. John Chrysostom, *Homilies on the Gospel of Matthew* 50.4: Do you wish to honor the body of Christ? Do not ignore him when he is naked. Do not pay him homage in the temple clad in silk only then to neglect him outside where he suffers cold and nakedness. He who said: "This is my body" is the same One who said: "You saw me hungry and you gave me no food" and "Whatever you did to the least of my brothers you did also to me." . . . What good is it if the eucharistic table is overloaded with golden chalices, when he is dying of hunger? Start by satisfying his hunger, and then with what is left you may adorn the altar as well.

SONG

AT THAT FIRST EUCHARIST
By William Henry Turton

At that first Eucharist before you died,
O Lord, you prayed that all be one in you;
At this our Eucharist again preside,
And in our hearts your law of love renew.
Thus may we all one Bread, one Body be;
Through this blest sacrament of unity.

For all your church, O Lord, we intercede;
O make our lack of charity to cease;
Draw us the nearer each to each we plead,
By drawing all to you, O Prince of Peace.
Thus may we all one Bread, one Body be;
Through this blest sacrament of unity.

We pray for those who wander from the
   fold;
O bring them back, Good Shepherd of the
   sheep.
Back to the faith which saints believed of old,
Back to the Church which still that faith does
   keep.
Thus may we all one Bread, one Body be;
Through this blest sacrament of unity.

QUESTIONS FOR REFLECTION
AND DISCUSSION

1. What does it mean to be "saved"? Do we often consider that we are not saved only *from* sin, but primar-
   ily *for* divine life?

2. Do you think most Catholics look upon the Church
   as God's family—or do they consider it just another
   voluntary association?

3. What can we do to improve the sense of family in
   our parish?

4. What strategies work best for exercising charity in
   parish life? How can we best avoid being distracted
   by our pet peeves and the real faults of other parishioners?

5. How does the Eucharist change us? How does it
   change you?

6. How can you and I make our devotion to the Trinity, and our experience of the Trinity, more personal?

7. What is a covenant? Why is it important?

For Further Reading

Scott Hahn, *First Comes Love: Finding Your Family in the Church and the Trinity* (New York: Doubleday, 2002).

Part 3, Chapter 4

Rite Makes Might
The Difference Mass Makes

SUMMARY AND KEY POINTS

- In the Mass we are warriors and witnesses, worshippers and martyrs.
- We take the Mass with us when we go out to the world.
- We bring the Mass with us when we go to Mass.

In the final chapter, we revisit the Mass, walking through it once again, but now applying what we have learned from our study of the Book of Revelation.

When we enter the church and bless ourselves with holy water, we renew our baptismal oath, and we are sworn in as witnesses—*martyres,* to use the Greek. Thus, we give testimony like the martyrs at heaven's altar.

We call upon God's name, which he has given us as our own.

We are sealed on our foreheads, like the saints in the Apocalypse. This has consequences for all the parts of the Mass, from the "Holy, Holy, Holy" to the Sign of Peace, from the "Lord, Have Mercy" to the dismissal. Our Communion is especially consequential.

Nor do the consequences end at the exits of the church. We carry our Communion into the world, and we bear testimony there. The Mass extends into our home and neighborhood and workplace, because we are really present there.

And we bring that world back to the Mass, next time we go, and we offer it again to God, placing it on the altar through the symbols of bread and wine, which earth has given and human hands have made.

The veil no longer divides us from the heavenly realities. God has accommodated himself to our human circumstances, our human needs. He has stooped down and spoken our language; he has lifted us up to hear his Word. He has recognized our hunger and filled it with himself.

In the Mass we find our fulfillment, given to us by him who created us. We will be restless until we rest in him. We will be hungry till we feed on him. We will know no satisfactory love or happiness till we possess his love and happiness and learn to share them freely.

SCRIPTURE

Revelation 21 and 22

DOCTRINE

St. Athanasius, *Festal Letter* 4.3: My beloved brethren, it is no temporal feast that we come to, but an eternal, heavenly feast. We do not display it in shadows; we approach it in reality.

St. John Chrysostom, *Homilies on Ephesians* 3: Look, I beg you: a royal table is set before you; angels minister at that table; the King himself is there—and will you stand gaping? . . . [Christ] has invited us to heaven, to the table of the great and wonderful King, and do we shrink and hesitate, instead of hastening and running to it?

SONG

AT THE LAMB'S HIGH FEAST
By Robert Campbell

At the Lamb's high feast we sing
Praise to our victorious King,
Who hath washed us in the tide
Flowing from his pierced side;
Praise we him, whose love divine
Gives his sacred Blood for wine,

Gives his Body for the feast,
Christ the victim, Christ the priest.

Where the Paschal blood is poured,
Death's dark angel sheathes his sword;
Israel's hosts triumphant go
Through the wave that drowns the foe.
Praise we Christ, whose blood was shed,
Paschal victim, Paschal bread;
With sincerity and love
Eat we manna from above.

Mighty victim from on high,
Hell's fierce powers beneath thee lie;
Thou hast conquered in the fight,
Thou hast brought us life and light:
Now no more can death appall,
Now no more the grave entrall;
Thou hast opened paradise,
And in thee thy saints shall rise.

Easter triumph, Easter joy,
Sin alone can this destroy;
From sin's power do thou set free
Souls newborn, O Lord, in thee.
Hymns of glory and of praise,
Risen Lord, to thee we raise;
Holy Father, praise to thee,
With the Spirit, ever be.

QUESTIONS FOR REFLECTION
AND DISCUSSION

1. How have your impressions of the Book of Revelation changed through this study?

2. How has your study of the Book of Revelation changed your experience of the Mass?

3. What more do you feel you need to change?

4. How are you better equipped to make such changes?

5. Are you any more aware of the importance of God's covenant, the work of the angels, and the snares of the devils? Are you better off for that awareness?

6. When do you foresee yourself returning to study or prayer with the Book of Revelation? Will it be in particular life circumstances, or in your routine personal study?

7. Is there a character you found most compelling in the Apocalypse? Who, and why?

For Further Reading

Scott Hahn, *Swear to God: The Promise and Power of the Sacraments* (New York: Doubleday, 2003), chapters 8–10.

Scott Hahn, *Letter and Spirit: From Written Text to Living Word in the Liturgy* (New York: Doubleday, 2005).